THIS SKETCHBOOK BELONGS TO ....

CONTACT ....

56 s

61 rare date D

41 Lincon cent

1960.D